KENDAL
IN OLD PHOTOGRAPHS

BARREL ORGAN IN WILDMAN STREET in 1902. At that time the County Hotel was known as the Railway and Commercial Hotel and had a side door into Wildman Street.

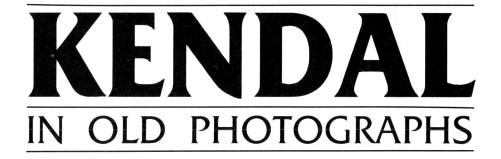

KENDAL
IN OLD PHOTOGRAPHS

COLLECTED BY
MARGARET AND PERCY DUFF

ALAN SUTTON

Alan Sutton Publishing Limited
Phoenix Mill · Far Thrupp · Stroud · Gloucestershire

First published 1992

British Library Cataloguing in Publication Data

Duff, Margaret
Kendal in Old Photographs
I. Title II. Duff, Percy
942.783

ISBN 0-7509-0108-X

Typeset in 9/10 Korinna.
Typesetting and origination by
Alan Sutton Publishing Limited.
Printed in Great Britain by
The Bath Press, Avon.

CONTENTS

INTRODUCTION

Kendal is picturesquely placed in the valley of the River Kent. It is surrounded by hills and the prospect of the town is unique, it consisting principally of buildings constructed of local limestone. The river flows through the centre of the town and is crossed by several bridges, one of which is a girder bridge built to celebrate Queen Victoria's Golden Jubilee. There are also three very fine old stone bridges and one of modern construction at the southern entrance to the town built recently to replace the Romney suspension bridge.

There was a Roman fort at Watercrook, just south of the town, but little is known of the activities of the inhabitants of the area until the Normans arrived in the eleventh century, when the Barony of Kendal was created, although there is part of a Saxon cross in the parish church. The Domesday Book, which was completed in 1088, surveyed the southern part of the old area of Westmorland and included 'Cherchebi Kendale', subsequently Kirkbie in Kendal.

The earliest document in existence is a charter in the Mayor's Parlour which was granted by Peter de Bruss III between 1247 and 1260 and which confirms certain rights and privileges granted to the inhabitants by his uncle William de Lancastre III, the Baron of Kendal between 1222 and 1246. This was probably confirmation of existing arrangements rather than a grant *de novo*. A copy of this earlier 'Seignorial Borough Charter' was found recently at Levens Hall, near Kendal, and it contains many interesting clauses setting out the areas where wood could be taken for building or fires, where and when animals could be grazed, and the use of the Lord's Mill and Oven. It is perhaps significant that the one trade referred to in this charter was cloth production. Agreement had to be made with the Lord's Fullers and Dyers.

The woollen industry played an important part in the local economy at that time. Tradition has it that the industry really flourished from the fourteenth century, when immigrants from Flanders were encouraged to settle in England, although it cannot be said with any certainty that any of the immigrants settled in Kendal. Kendal cloth was referred to in a statute of Richard II in 1390, and administration of the woollen industry was set out in the later Borough Charters of 1575, 1636 and 1684. It was the backbone of the town's wealth until the Industrial Revolution, when the trade moved away to the factories being erected in Lancashire and Yorkshire. Cloth made in Kendal was generally of coarse quality and worn by the working classes or exported to America and the West Indies where it was used to clothe the slaves. Very little of this type of cloth has been preserved. The Pattern Book in possession of the Town Council, which was used by a Packman, or commercial traveller, for showing cloth merchants' samples at the end of the eighteenth century, contains a great variety of samples and is unique.

In connection with the woollen trade, Kendal was noted for a dark olive shade of green known universally as Kendal Green. It is mentioned in Shakespeare's *King Henry IV* by Falstaff and Prince Henry as the colour worn by 'three misbegotten knaves', and Sir Walter Scott mentions the colour in his *Lay of the Last Minstrel*, where he refers to 'the Kendal Archers all in green'.

The town's coat of arms reflects the importance of the woollen industry. The shield is quartered with what are now accepted as wool hooks and teasels, and was first used officially in 1629 on a silver tankard presented to the Town Council. A rough drawing of the coat of arms was shown on Speed's Map of 1614, and he has been credited with its invention, but it may have been in use before that date. The latin motto is translated loosely as 'Wool is my Bread'.

Proximity to the border with Scotland meant that Kendal was always subject to invasion and depredation by the Scots who, even down to the middle of the eighteenth century, were always a constant terror to the inhabitants of Kendal. In 1201, and again in the reign of Edward I, and at various other times the town was attacked in force. One result was that the men of Kendal became expert in the use of the arrow and the practices of war and they wiped out old scores with the Scots on Flodden Field. The exploits of the Kendal bowmen there brought them considerable distinction. However, they did not altogether deter the Scots who entered the town in the 'Rebellion' of 1715 and again in 1745. On the latter occasion the Young Pretender, Prince Charles Edward, lodged at 95 Strick-landgate, and his father was proclaimed King at the Market Cross, but his triumph was short lived as the Duke of Cumberland soon chased the Scots across the border.

As the centre of a large rural area, Kendal has always been an important market town and this was recognized as long ago as 1189 when a charter was obtained from King Richard the Lion Heart by the Baron of Kendal granting him the right to hold a market in Kendal on Saturdays. The Baron was with the King in Rouen on a Crusade at the time and, as the King was probably short of money, the Baron would have had to pay for his charter. It is likely that Kendal was a market centre long before the charter was granted. The charter itself has long since disappeared but it was recorded at the time and photographs have been supplied by the Public Record Office. Over the centuries other charters have been granted and street markets are now held on Wednesdays and Saturdays.

The first Royal Charter incorporating the inhabitants as a Borough was granted by Queen Elizabeth I in 1575. The chief citizen was an alderman and he had to be preceded on all civic occasions by two Sergeants of Mace. Under this charter the Town Council adopted planning powers and decreed that all new building and alterations and improvements would be subject to their approval.

It was not until a second charter was granted by king Charles I in 1636 that the office of mayor was created. The charter stated that the mayor should be preceded at all times by a bearer of the sovereign's sword. These three symbols of power granted by the sovereigns are the most valuable of the town's regalia and are carried by officers clad in Kendal Green on all civic occasions. The second charter also appointed the mayor as the Clerk of the Market.

Towards the end of the reign of King Charles II these two charters were surrendered and a new one was granted in 1684. This charter was brought from London by the Town Clerk and was received with great pomp and ceremony. This was the form of government until the Municipal Corporations Act of 1835.

Under the provisions of the Local Government Act of 1972 Kendal lost its status as a Municipal Borough from 1 April 1974, but as a result of representations made to the appropriate government department the Town Council was allowed to continue with greatly reduced powers but with no loss of dignity. The office of mayor is still greatly respected and traditional parades and ceremonies continue as they have done for many years.

Kendal Castle, at one time the home of the Parr family, is generally accepted as the birthplace of Katherine Parr who was the sixth and only wife to survive of King Henry VIII. Her personal prayer book is in the possession of the Town Council. The castle has been a ruin for several centuries but her name has been adopted by one of the schools and Queen Katherine Street and Parr Street are at the base of Castle Hill. The famous portrait painter George Romney served his apprenticeship in Kendal and married a Kendal girl. Several of his paintings are in the Mayor's Parlour and on public display at Abbot Hall Art Gallery. His name has also been perpetuated in the names of several streets. More recently Kendal became the adopted home of the famous Lake District author and artist Alfred Wainwright, and much of his original work is on display in the museum.

Stricklandgate was the subject of John Macadam's first experiment in road making in 1824. At that time he was employed by the local Turnpike Trust. His method was to drain the subsoil and then render it impervious with a covering of broken angular stones. His experiment was not popular and the local farmers alleged that the sharp stones lamed their horses beyond recovery. Certain citizens wrote to the *Westmorland Gazette* saying they were disgusted with his road making and wished that he had carried out his experiment on the top of Shap. Nevertheless, when tar became available as a binding material his name was perpetuated in 'Tarmacadam'.

For over one hundred years Kendal has been known as the centre for the Mary Wakefield Music Festival. The first festival was held by Mary Wakefield on the tennis court at Sedgwick House. It has now become so popular that it is necessary to take over all the suitable halls in the town to accommodate the orchestral playing and choral singing during the period of the festival. Although it is an entirely amateur festival for the people of Kendal and the surrounding towns and villages, singers and conductors of national fame are invited to take part.

Kendal is now a busy market town of approximately 25,000 inhabitants. It is well served by the M6 and the main West Coast railway line. It has a strong varied commercial and industrial base and many attractions for tourists. It has been known for many years as 'The Gateway to the Lakes'.

Transport

HOTEL BUSES in the forecourt of Kendal station. It was the practice to meet all trains and tout for business for the hotels.

A LEYLAND LION 'K' BUS near Tithe Barn Cottages. The driver is Tom Stilling and conductor Arnold Stilling. The Kendal Motor Bus Company operated local services in Kendal and the surrounding areas during the 1920s and was taken over by Ribble Motor Services in 1930. At that time they had a fleet of thirty-two buses.

CUSTOMERS OF THE SEVEN STARS in Stricklandgate about to leave for an outing. The Seven Stars was demolished in 1989 and the site is now part of the Black Hall Yard shopping precinct.

PRIOR TO THE PURCHASE OF THIS MODEL 'T' FORD the Steam Laundry had used horse-drawn traps. John Greenbank was selected as the driver to move from reins to steering wheel.

T. & H. RICHMOND WERE GROCERS and had their shop in Stricklandgate. The photograph shows the ladies who operated the delivery service when the men were away during the First World War.

MR CLAYTON HAD JUST TAKEN DELIVERY OF HIS NEW VEHICLE from Messrs Atkinson & Griffin in Kirkland. The space for carrying meat is small and was probably a local conversion.

THE WESTMORLAND LAUNDRY was in Ann Street, and after the First World War, under the ownership of Isaac Braithwaite and Son, became drysalters and laundry chemical specialists.

THE SECTION OF THE CANAL BETWEEN LANCASTER AND KENDAL was opened by a grand aquatic procession on 18 June 1819 and brought great benefit to the town. The *Herbert S. Kent* was crewed by man, wife and dog and registered at Preston.

THE PROSPERITY OF THE CANAL WAS SHORT LIVED. When the railway reached Kendal in 1846 both passenger and goods traffic virtually ceased but coal was brought to the gasworks and canal head for the next hundred years. On Whit Tuesdays the barges were cleaned and lined with hessian and used for the Sunday School outings to Levens Park. It was thought desirable to take the children away from the evils of the Kendal Races which were held on that day.

THE 'K' CYCLE WORKS were in Yard 10, Stricklandgate, and were described as Braithwaite Bros, Cycle Manufacturers. They assembled bicycles and sold them under the 'K' label.

IT WAS THE CUSTOM for the farm hands and farm girls to come into Kendal on Saturday nights and leave their bicycles down the yard. In those days there was very little thieving and they were quite safe and were always there at home time. After sampling the pleasures at the inns in Kendal it might have been a problem finding your own bike.

GOODS ARRIVING BY TRAIN were distributed throughout the area by horse-drawn carts. Many of the horses were familiar with their rounds and knew where to stop. When off duty, the horses were allowed to graze on Beezon Field adjoining the river. The photograph shows the final parade, which was attended by the mayor, Alderman George Jackson, in 1949. Delivery was then taken over by mechanical horses.

OXENHOLME is the junction where the Kendal and Windermere branch joins the West Coast main line to Scotland. This photograph was taken before 1923 in the days of the London and North Western Railway. The Mexican-looking gentleman on the left on the back row looks rather out of place.

A LONDON AND NORTH WESTERN TRAIN of six-wheeled coaches drawing into Kendal station from Windermere hauled by one of F.W. Webb's 2–4–0 Jumbos.

A LONDON AND NORTH WESTERN TRAIN at Oxenholme, headed by 'Jubilee' class 4–4–0 4-cylinder compound No. 1918 *Renown*.

A MIXED GOODS TRAIN waiting for the banker at Oxenholme: engine No. 44505 'Standard' class 4F 0–6–0.

STANIER 2–6–4 'TANKS' CLASS 4P at Oxenholme Sheds. These sheds provided motive power for the Windermere branch and banking engines for heavy goods trains as far as Grayrigg.

THE RAILWAY BRIDGE on the Greyhound Hill on the road to Sedbergh out of Kendal had cast iron plates on both sides commemorating the opening of the 'Lancaster & Carlisle Railway 1846'. The photograph was taken in 1956 before the plates were removed and the bridge strengthened under the West Coast Electrification Scheme.

THE FIRST TRAINLOAD OF TRACTORS arriving in Kendal after the Second World War. In the background is the busy goods yard and depot. At that time the railways were still the main goods carriers. The goods yard is now closed and has been developed as an industrial and commercial area.

KENDAL STATION, looking south towards Oxenholme. The buildings on the left have been demolished. The line is now single track and the station facilities are reduced to an unmanned stone shelter.

THE CREW AND OTHER OFFICIALS were proud to pose by this London and North Western Railway Ramsbottom 'Newton' class 2–4–0 No. 1532 *Hampden* outside the sheds at Oxenholme.

COACHES FROM HARRY SIMPSON'S LIVERY STABLES at the County Mews in Sandes Avenue. The building was converted into the Palladium Cinema in the early 1930s but is now occupied by residential flats using the original name 'County Mews'.

BEFORE THE ARRIVAL OF THE MOTOR LORRY a network of carriers operated from the various inns in Kendal to the surrounding towns and villages. The photograph shows William Burrows, who operated a service to Sedbergh on Tuesdays, Thursdays and Saturdays. Parcels could be left at the Angel or the Woolpack.

HORSE-DRAWN CARRIAGE waiting outside James Douglas's shop at 8 Stricklandgate. This is now a shoe shop.

ALEXANDER'S TABLE WATERS.

AVENUE WORKS.

J. ALEXANDER & SONS manufactured mineral and table waters in syphon and bottle at their works in Sandes Avenue, and these were delivered locally by horse and cart.

ATKINSON & GRIFFIN supplied the famous Darracq and Clement Talbot motor cars in addition to Ford cars and vans. Model 'T' Fords were not cheap. The firm moved from these premises in Highgate to larger premises in Kirkland. For many years this shop was the Ribble Motor Services office but is now used as a showroom for horticultural machinery.

GILBERT PARKINSON WITH LEN ELLWOOD outside his premises in Kent Street in 1931. Any make of motor cycle could be supplied but his main agency was for Ariels.

J. CHAPLOW & SONS OF HELSINGTON MILLS maintained a fleet of traction engines for heavy haulage, agricultural work, and road making. The engine in the photograph is taking on water at the horse trough at Highfield on Windermere Road. The firm is still in operation as road contractors.

THE WESTMORLAND COUNTY COUNCIL STEAM ROLLER at work with driver Matthew James and his mate.

SEVERAL LOCAL HOTELS RAN BUSES for the convenience of their customers. The King's Arms bus is on the New Road. The hotel literature claimed that the bus met all trains at Kendal station.

A NEW DELIVERY VAN for the Westmorland Laundering Company standing in the yard at their premises in Ann Street.

CRAGHILL AND COMPANY operated a Battery Service Station in Sandes Avenue. Early radios had wet batteries which had to be charged regularly and this Trojan van was used to collect and deliver batteries.

THE MEMBERS OF KENDAL TOWN COUNCIL, at the invitation of the mayor, Alderman Monkhouse, went on an outing to Keswick and Greystoke Castle on 6 July 1911. After taking the train to Windermere the party continued by motor charabanc to Keswick. The photograph shows the party resting at the summit of Dunmail Raise.

EDWARD BOUNDY was an early car dealer who had premises in Yard 56, Stramongate. It was his practice to send photographs of the cars he had for sale to possible customers.

ON THE OUTBREAK OF THE FIRST WORLD WAR a wave of patriotism swept across the country and this photograph shows a car which toured the town appealing to local young men to enlist for King and Country.

THE JUNGLE CAFE on the A6 north of Kendal on the approach to Shap Fells. This was a recognized halt for heavy vehicle drivers before the construction of the M6. The road over Shap Fells was frequently blocked by snow in winter and the lorries congregated at the Jungle and also back in Kendal until the road was cleared.

THE RAILWAY BRIDGE AT LONGPOOL caused many problems and high loads had to be diverted by Burneside. After the Second World War the Borough Council carried out a major improvement scheme, lowering the road. The contractors were W.H. Ainsworth & Co. Ltd.

A COACH PARTY about to return to Preston after stopping for refreshment at the Ring o' Bells in Kirkland.

COMPETITORS in the Automobile Club's 1,000 mile trial pausing at Green Road after ascending the House of Correction Hill on 1 May 1900. The purpose of the trial was to advance the automobile movement in the United Kingdom. In the rules it stated: 'On the open road no speed in excess of the legal limit of 12 miles an hour will be recognised and in towns any speed in excess of 8 miles an hour is prohibited.'

Recreation

KENDAL GREEN SCHOOL SQUADRON SWIMMING TEAM in 1927. Miss Ellwood is in the centre.

CONTRACTORS AT WORK refurbishing the interior of St George's Theatre in the early 1930s. The Kendal Amateur Operatic and Dramatic Societies used the theatre for their annual shows but its main use was as a cinema until bingo became popular. The building was destroyed by fire on 10 February 1992.

THE FOYER of St George's Theatre where second house patrons waited for the first house to 'come out'.

RUGBY UNION FOOTBALL started in Kendal in 1871 and quickly became very popular. Several teams were formed but the most famous was Kendal Hornets. The photograph shows the team for the 1876/77 season. The name was derived from the black jerseys with amber stripe generally worn by the team.

KENDAL CRICKET CLUB, 1926. Back row, left to right: F. Hindle, W. Hewitson, H. Hall (professional), -?-, W.F. Pennington, J.T. Lowe, -?-. Middle row: R.R. Dawson, T.D. Page, G.H. Wileman, E.C. Wroth (captain), W. Leather, J. Heaps. Front row: F.S. Ellwood, E. Jones.

KENDAL RUGBY UNION FOOTBALL TEAM, 1922/23 season, on Maudes Meadow in front of St Thomas's church. Back row, left to right: P. Winder, S. Alexander, T. Mark, F. Carradus, T. Carradus, E. Wilson, A. Langhorn, J.D. Blackburn, J.A. Wilcock. Middle row: H. Simm, D. Haigh, R. Pickthall, H. Wills (captain), J.H. Braithwaite, A. Raynor, J. Thompson, T. Philipson. Front row: E. Johnson, S. Bewsher, W. Langhorne, G. Hodgson.

NETHERFIELD FOOTBALL CLUB, Westmorland Cup winners 1931/32. Back row, left to right: H. Wilkinson, L. Barwise, R. Fawcett, W. Ward, W. Postlethwaite, H. Hutton, T. Mackie. Front row, left to right: J.H. Tyson (Chairman), Joe Hillbeck, G. Wallace, F. Thompson (Capt.), Jack Hillbeck, J. Wilson, R. Brennand (Secretary).

FLYING CIRCUSES made regular visits to Longlands on Appleby Road in the 1930s. In addition to flying displays and acrobatics, it was possible to have a short trip over the town for 5s. The photograph shows local children watching the mechanics at work.

MISS DAY IN HER CANOE on the River Kent just below Nether Bridge. The Day family owned a foundry in Kendal.

CUMBERLAND AND WESTMORLAND WREST-LING is always a major event at Lake District sports. Here a bout is taking place in Maudes Meadow with Beech Hill Terrace in the background.

THE SERPENTINE WOODS, part of the Fell Estate, have always been popular with local people, particularly children.

THE MOST POPULAR DANCE BAND in 1927 was conducted by Arthur Higginson, seen on the left at the piano. Dancing was very popular, not only in the Town Hall but in the halls and institutes in the surrounding villages.

THE DOMINOES TROUPE provided entertainment under the guidance of Stan Robinson, seen in the dress suit. Back row, left to right: Doris Smith, Pat Brogden, Stan Robinson, Mr Hunt, -?-, Joan Moorhouse. Front row: Rene Stables, Joan Shepherd, Elsie Richardson, Mary Fleming.

THERE WAS KEEN COMPETITION to join the Dinky Kids Concert Party which flourished just before and after the Second World War.

PROFESSOR AND MADAME AIREY had their Victorian Academy of Dancing in Entry Lane at what is now the Red Cross headquarters. Plain, artistic, and fancy dancing was taught. The photograph taken in 1920 shows, back row, left to right: Moyra Doherty, Eva Monkhouse, Annie Noble, and Madame Airey. Front row: Beatrice Greenbank, Marjorie Braithwaite, and Marjorie Noble.

UNDER ANCIENT CHARTERS two fairs are held each year on common land on the New Road. Before the Second World War they were known as hiring fairs as they were held when the farm lads and lassies were hired for another term. No doubt a good proportion of the money earned in the previous term found its way into the pockets of the showmen.

'THE MANX WALKING KING' pushed his wheelbarrow from Lands End to John o' Groats in thirty days in 1906. He is seen passing Millward's tailors shop at 90 Stricklandgate.

KENDAL AMATEUR SWIMMING CLUB TEAM won the Carlisle and District Swimming Club's water polo Challenge Shield in 1925. Back row, left to right: John Nicholson (secretary), Bevan Tyson, Albert Roth, Bruce Alexander, George Humphreys, Mr Cummings (baths superintendent). Front row: Norman Simm, William Kendal, Sam Martindale.

NETHERFIELD CHOIR on the sports ground at Parkside Road in the early 1930s.

OFFICIALS OF THE MARY WAKEFIELD WESTMORLAND MUSIC FESTIVAL in May 1905. In the centre is Sir Henry Wood with Mary Wakefield on the left and Agnes Argles on the right.

THE KENDAL AMATEUR OPERATIC SOCIETY was founded in 1913 for the study and performance of operas and musical plays. The photograph shows the company on the stage at St George's Theatre in 1930 during the performance of *The Vagabond King*.

APART FROM A BREAK OF EIGHT YEARS between 1939 and 1946, the society has succeeded in carrying out its primary object. In 1938 the cast of *The Belle of New York* posed for this group photograph. Back row, left to right: Leslie Marshall, Gladys Bickerton, Jack Beck, Arthur Burns. Middle row: Elsie Duff, Pat Brogden, Alan Jenner, Rene Reddish, Tommy Allen, Winnie Hogg, John Wright. Front row: Fred Taylor, Arthur Camm, Leonard Allen.

THE WESTMORLAND MOTOR CLUB is one of the oldest in the country, founded in 1910 as a result of a meeting of motor cycling enthusiasts held in the Commercial Hotel in Kendal in January of that year. The first event was a hill climb on Shap Fells on Good Friday and the photograph shows the competitors at the start.

BRYAN JEFFERYS WITH HIS TRIUMPH being checked by a club official at the start of a road trial before the First World War. He returned to civilian life after losing a leg and continued to compete on a Norton with a sidecar. The photograph was taken on Milnthorpe Road at the top of what is known locally as Orphans Home Hill.

FRANK IRELAND THE DENTIST with his Scott and sidecar on the weighbridge on the New Road at the start of a Westmorland Motor Club trial.

THE 'K' CYCLE CLUB about to set out on a run. At the end of the last century, before the arrival of the internal combustion engine, cycling was very popular with both sexes.

IT USED TO BE THE CUSTOM to congregate on the Castle Hill on Easter Monday. There were various stalls and the children rolled their 'pache' eggs, hard boiled eggs painted or stained in various colours.

THE HEAVY HORSE SECTION at the Westmorland Agricultural Show in 1906.

THE AGRICULTURAL SHOW was held at one time on what is now the cricket field. The buildings which fronted on to Shap Road and Pump Yard have been demolished.

E. RICHARDSON & COMPANY'S STAND at the agricultural show. This company specialized in Plain and Fancy Coopering at their works in the Old Shambles.

THE KENDAL TOWN SIX-A-SIDE TEAM which won the Kendal Friendly Society Gala 1885, the Northern Counties Competition at Barrow 1885, and Lancaster Gala 1886. Standing at the rear: I. Alexander. Centre row, left to right: W. Banks, R. Beard, I. Amer. Front row: E. Hoggarth, R. Chorley.

Kendal Victoria Bowling Club.
1910.

THE KENDAL VICTORIA BOWLING CLUB was most definitely an all male preserve in 1910. The club continues to prosper but now admits lady members.

THE AMBULANCE CYCLE PARADE on Aynam Road. It would appear that toreadors on foot or on horseback qualified for entry.

SPRING, SUMMER AND AUTUMN IN THE CYCLE PARADE. Winter was probably not thought to be suitable.

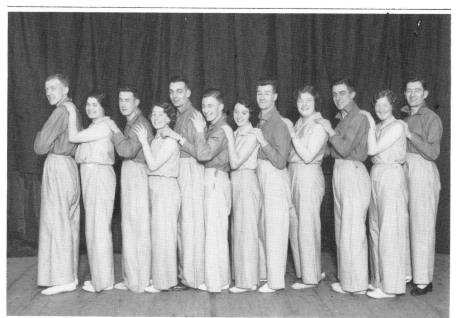

THE 'Y TOCS' CONCERT PARTY consisted of girls from the YWCA and men from the Toc H. In the 1930s they were in great demand in the surrounding villages as well as at the YWCA Hall in Kendal. Left to right: Miles Coulton, Myfanwy Hall, Harry Reed, Elsie Duff, Stan Walling, -?-, -?-, Stanley Sill, -?-, Billy Martin, -?-, John Wright.

THE ZION DRAMA GROUP performing in the church hall in Highgate in 1959. The group is still active and presents at least one play a year.

THE FIRST GOLF CLUB IN KENDAL was formed in 1891 and played on the disused race course adjacent to Scout Scar. A second club was formed in 1893 and because of its situation was called the Cunswick Golf Club. In 1897 it obtained the use of eighty-eight acres of land near the Serpentine Woods and changed its name to the Serpentine Golf Club. In 1907 the race course club was absorbed and the Kendal Golf Club was formed. A member is shown driving from the first tee, the length 243 yards.

LADIES WERE ENCOURAGED TO JOIN and as early as 1893 arrangements were made for a ladies dressing room. The elegant group of members is standing in front of the first corrugated iron club house.

THE EMPLOYEES FROM THE 'K' SHOE WORKS organized an annual fête in the 1930s to raise money to support the Westmorland County Hospital which at that time relied on voluntary subscriptions. There was a procession through the town to the cricket field on Parkside Road where the 'K' Queen paraded with her retainers to be crowned.

A TYPICAL FLOAT IN THE PROCESSION. Most of the floats were horse-drawn.

SECTION THREE

Floods, Public Works and Public Buildings

THE LAST BIG FLOOD was in 1954 when the water was level with the deck of the Romney Suspension Bridge. This bridge has been replaced by a new road bridge but a scheme is under consideration for its re-erection at Aikrigg Avenue.

THE WATER NEARLY FILLED THE MIDDLE ARCH of Nether Bridge in 1954. The Cock and Dolphin Inn can be seen in the background.

THERE HAVE BEEN THREE SERIOUS FLOODS in the last hundred years, in 1898, 1927 and 1954. This lorry is coming along Ann Street in 1927.

LAYING THE NEW SEWER IN KIRKLAND. The Borough Surveyor, Mr R.H. Clucas, stands on the right next to Councillor Edmondson, Chairman of the Committee. The properties on the right have been demolished as far as the Ring o' Bells, the end of which can be seen in the background.

THE RIVER WAS VERY LOW when this photograph was taken of the main sewer being laid in the river bed. The Castle Mills race is on the left.

THE MAIN SEWER outside the Grammar School in Lound Road. In the background is Tudor House, standing at the junction of Burton Road and Natland Road, the site of the old Toll Bar. The new Romney Bridge crosses the river here and a roundabout has been constructed.

EXTENDING THE CABLE in front of St Thomas's church for Kendal Corporation Electricity Department.

VIEW FROM THE HEIGHTS OF THE HOUSE OF CORRECTION on Windermere Road. An imposing building surrounded by high walls, it was closed as a civil prison in 1894 but was used for military prisoners until after the Boer war.

THE PRISON YARD WITH THE PUMP. The building has been demolished and houses erected on the site. Very little of the prison can now be identified.

THE IMPOSING MAIN DOOR TO THE PRISON.

THE INTERIOR OF THE PRISON. Very little seems to have changed in the design!

THE SPACIOUS READING ROOM at the Public Library in Stricklandgate. Chairs were provided to read the magazines at the tables but it was necessary to stand to read the newspapers round the wall. This area is now part of the general library, with racks of books. Space for reading newspapers and magazines is very limited.

AT THE END OF THE LAST CENTURY the demand for water was growing and a new reservoir was commenced in 1895 at Fisher Tarn and completed in 1900. The cost was £60,000, of which £30,000 was left as a legacy to the town by the late mayor, Alderman Bindloss. Work is proceeding on the dam. North West Water no longer use this source of supply.

"CIMENT FONDU" ROAD BEING LAID AT NETHER BRIDGE. KENDAL 20TH OCT. 1924.

NETHER BRIDGE connects Kirkland and Netherfield, and during its long life it has been widened and strengthened many times. In 1924 an experimental 'Cement Fondu' surface was laid.

THE KENDAL AND DISTRICT HOUSING SOCIETY developed an estate adjoining houses erected by the Borough Council under the Housing of the Working Classes Act 1890 in the late 1920s. A large crowd assembled at the opening of Nos 5 and 7 Underley Road.

THE PUBLIC LIBRARY stood at the entrance to the Market Place. The lane to the right hand side was called Mercers Lane and that on the left Cheapside. A lamp can be seen above the entrance to the library which opened in 1891 when the Public Libraries Act was adopted by the Borough Council.

THE LIBRARY WAS DEMOLISHED in 1909 when the present Carnegie Library was opened in Stricklandgate. The entrance to the Market Place remained as an open space until the War Memorial was erected in 1921.

SECTION FOUR

Industry and Commerce

GIRLS WORKING in the closing room at the 'K' Shoe Factory at Netherfield, 1892.

THE MAKING DEPARTMENT AT NETHERFIELD.

THE WELTING SECTION, 'K' SHOES.

M. CROFT & SON'S SHOWROOM AND WORKSHOPS were in Wildman Street. They were major suppliers of agricultural implements and this photograph was taken when horses were the motive power. In the background is the scaffolding erected by the builders extending the County Hotel. The showroom is now occupied by Provincial Insurance plc.

CRAGHILL'S EMPLOYEES in the garage forecourt in Stricklandgate. The two hand-operated pumps have long since disappeared and a new showroom has been erected further back from the road with a workshop in the rear. They no longer provide a magneto or battery service, but are agents for Fiat cars.

BRAITHWAITE & CO. LTD, Kendal hand-loom linsey weavers. Back row, left to right: William Beaumont (80), Anthony Troughton, Mr H.B. Braithwaite, John Troughton, Benjamin Thompson. Front row, left to right: George Major, Robert Dixon, William Bousfield (87), Thomas Mounsey, John Garnett.

MILL GIRLS WITH THE CHARGE HANDS outside Braithwaite's Woollen Mill in Highgate at the turn of the century. Mr George Foster Braithwaite lived at Hawesmead and was mayor six times. He also owned the mill at Mealbank.

JOHN C. KENNEDY'S PREMISES were in the Old Shambles. A fine example of their work can be seen leaning against the wall. The gentlemen's toilet gates were for the Borough Council Health Department.

WORKMEN AT THE GASWORKS on Parkside Road which were purchased by the Borough Council in 1894 and remained in the Council's possession until the Gas Industry was nationalized. Gas was supplied to Burneside and Staveley in addition to the town of Kendal.

THE FIRM OF GILBERT GILKES AND GORDON LTD was founded in 1857 and manufactured turbines, hydraulic machinery and pumps. In their catalogue for 1911 they claim to manufacture appliances for the mechanical and electrical transmission of power.

BRAITHWAITES assembled 'K' Cycles at their works in Yard 10, Stricklandgate. A variety of models are shown on their stand at the Manchester Show in 1897, some of them fitted with 'tubeless' tyres. Mr William Rushworth of Deansgate was the sole agent for Manchester.

ISAAC BRAITHWAITE AND SON, DRYSALTERS were founded in 1713. The photograph is of a show stand exhibiting laundry supplies.

LAUNDRY MACHINES manufactured by Isaac Braithwaite and Son, Engineers Ltd, awaiting despatch from their works which were on Shap Road.

PRESSING COLLARS AND CUFFS.

J.T. ILLINGWORTH & SONS, TOBACCO AND SNUFF MANUFACTURERS moved to Aynam Mills from Sandes Avenue after the First World War. The photographs show snuff and twist being prepared. Unfortunately, this old established business ceased when the factory was destroyed by fire.

J.W. HOWIE'S WORKMEN in the builder's yard in Bridge Street. Experienced men were kept for drainage, fixing kitchen ranges, parlour grates, tiled hearths, and tiling. This area has been cleared and is now a car park for Gilbert Gilkes and Gordon Ltd.

H. WILLS AND J. COWARD in Howie's yard. The blocks of stone were for Lloyds Bank in Finkle Street.

ROBINSON'S TIMBER MERCHANTS' HORSES outside the Rifleman's Arms on Greenside. The stables were at the top of Queen Street.

MR JAMES CROPPER bought the mills at Burneside and Cowan Head in 1845 and erected the mill at Bowston in 1874. The firm has produced quality paper for nearly 150 years. Modern machinery has long since replaced that shown in the photograph.

SECTION FIVE

Shops and Inns

THERE HAVE BEEN MANY CHANGES to the properties on this site in Stricklandgate, opposite the War Memorial. Townley and Taylor specialized in Hornby and Meccano, and there was the Scotch Wool Shop. These were demolished to make way for a Co-operative supermarket, which in turn has given way to a large NORWEB showroom. The entrance on the right was known as White Lion Yard and was the location of a common lodging house.

MR FARRER standing outside his Tea and Coffee Warehouse. The front of the shop remains the same today and a large selection of teas and coffees is available. There is also a small coffee shop. His advertisement at the time of Queen Victoria's Diamond Jubilee claimed, 'In quality it is high. In price it is low.'

WATSON BROTHERS claimed to be complete outfitters. Their shop in Highgate was demolished and set back and rebuilt as Lonsdale House. The site is now occupied by Greenwoods and Rumbelows.

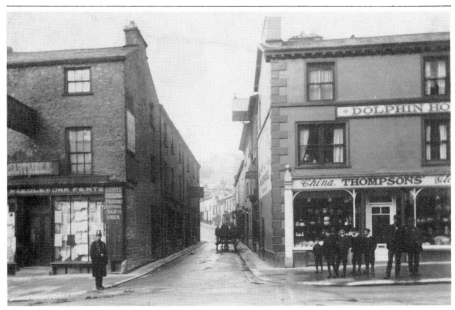

ALLHALLOWS LANE. This was the main road to Ulverston and was known at one time as Cripplegate. Most of the lane was widened in 1862 and Cartmell's shop and the properties in the remaining narrow section were demolished in 1914. Dolphin House was probably at one time an old inn.

JAMES WILSON'S HAIRDRESSERS SHOP at 14 and 16 Stricklandgate. The bedrooms of the King's Arms Hotel extended over the shop.

THIS SHOP IN KIRKLAND has changed occupation many times since this photograph was taken of Mr C.R. Airey's staff.

MRS WALKER outside her shop at 37 Castle Street. Until the big supermarkets arrived, small grocers shops were common throughout the town.

THOMAS EDWARD LANGHORNE had a Boot and Shoe Warehouse on the New Road before moving to 4 Market Place after the First World War. This photograph was taken in 1922. The business ceased in the 1980s.

DANIEL QUIGGIN'S SHOP was at 86 Stricklandgate, at the end of Library Road. He was described as a 'Practical Sugar Boiler and Confectioner' and made pure sweets, invalid toffee and Mona cough drops. Later he also made Kendal Mint Cake. The shop was demolished to widen the entrance to a car park and supermarket.

MR W.C. SHAW was an Ironmonger and Tinsmith who had this shop at 40 Highgate and his works in Stricklandgate. His advertisement in 1930 offered 'Lamps, Kerbs, Garden Tools, Cutlery, Cartridges and Farmers' Requisites'. Shortly afterwards he sold the shop to F.W. Woolworth and Company.

THE KENDAL CO-OPERATIVE SOCIETY prospered between the wars, and in addition to several grocery and butchers shops in Kendal it had a café and branches in the surrounding villages. The photograph shows the Co-operative properties at the junction of Ann Street and Wildman Street. The arrival of the supermarket sounded the death knell of the Kendal Co-operative and the society has ceased to operate.

THE KENDAL CO-OPERATIVE SOCIETY was founded in 1812. In addition to the grocery and butchers branches there was this central department at Waterloo House for drapery, furniture, hardware, footwear, etc.

HENRY DODD was a butcher at 34 Stramongate, adjoining the entrance to St George's Theatre. This entrance has now disappeared.

J. MOORE ON BRANTHWAITE BROW claimed to be a Practical Watchmaker, Jeweller, Optician, etc. The front of the shop was made of cast iron plates, a unique method of construction which still stands today.

THIS SHOP at 54 Stricklandgate has changed hands many times, but most recently it was McCormacks Home Furnishers until it was purchased by Halfords. On the right there are hooped carts in the Woolpack Yard.

STAFF OUTSIDE THE MAYPOLE SHOP at 19 Finkle Street in May 1939.

MRS MARY BOWSHER supplied fish, poultry and ice, and was licensed to sell game when this photograph was taken of her shop at 24 Finkle Street in 1904.

W. FLEET'S SHOP at 39 Allhallows Lane was typical of the small independent grocer who gave personal service and employed an errand boy to deliver the orders.

THE STAFF OF T. LEIGHTON & SON outside the shop at 48 Highgate. In the left hand window there is a fine selection of bacon and hams. This firm had a motor lorry to deliver the weekly orders.

BATEMANS at 29 Stramongate was described as Grocers, Provision Merchants and Confectioners. They were renowned for their home-made fudge and toffee.

SEVERAL FIRMS MADE KENDAL MINT CAKE but Wipers claimed to be the original. Their shop, at 72 Stricklandgate, now the Gas Showrooms, was well covered with advertisements for their products.

MRS FLORENCE TANNER at the door of her dressmakers shop at 29 Market Place.

THE LONGPOOL GROCERY BRANCH of the Kendal Co-operative Society.

JOSEPH SAWYERS at 12 Finkle Street was a dealer in all kinds of toys, fancy baskets, purses, bags, brushes and bird cages. This firm is remembered today because of the large number of postcards it supplied; they can be seen in the display cabinets mounted on the wall. These premises are now occupied by the Trustee Savings Bank.

GEORGE HIGGIN in the doorway of his ironmongery shop at 7–9 Stramongate in the 1920s. This was the town house of the Bellingham family of Burneside and Levens. The premises are now used as a bookshop.

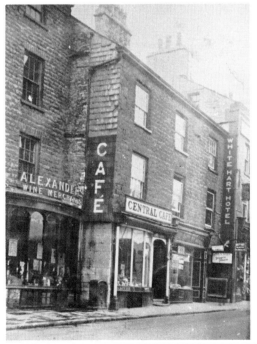

THESE THREE SHOPS are Nos 4, 6 and 8 Highgate, and are difficult to recognize now because 4 and 6 have been rebuilt as part of Mumford House. They are occupied at present by shops selling jumpers, jewellery and cards respectively.

THE GROUND FLOOR OF THE KENDAL HOTEL has now been converted into a building society office. The shop next door was occupied by Fred Long, a tobacconist. Fred was a great sportsman and captain of both rugby and cricket teams. His shop has been combined with the corner shop and is now occupied by a national firm of jewellers.

MR WILLIAM CROPPER standing at the door of the Wheatsheaf inn in Kirkland.

THE GOLDEN BALL INN, Allhallows Lane. The ground floor is now occupied by Greenbanks as a shop selling fruit, vegetables and flowers.

THE SHAKESPEARE INN in Highgate in 1938. The *News Chronicle* poster says 'Chamberlain Flying to Hitler'. His efforts gained us a year's grace to prepare for war.

THE SEVEN STARS HOTEL IN STRICKLANDGATE. This was a Whitwell Mark's Hotel selling Kendal-brewed ales and stout. The words 'Good Stabling' inscribed on the arch encouraged farmers to leave their horses and traps before the era of the motor car. This hotel has been demolished and the site is now part of the Black Hall Yard shopping arcade.

THE ANGEL HOTEL next to the Town Hall was the favourite overnight stopping place for commercial travellers when they came by train. Because of complaints the Town Hall carillon did not play at 3 a.m. The hotel has closed and the property been converted into shops.

THE FLEECE INN at 14 Highgate
(formerly The Golden Fleece)
was established in the seven-
teenth century. The front has
changed little over the years
and the names show the connection of the town with the
wool trade.

HENRY WIPER WITH HIS WIFE AND STAFF at the
entrance to the Cock and Dolphin in Kirkland at the turn of the century. This public
house has been completely rebuilt.

SECTION SIX

Military, Police and Fire Brigade

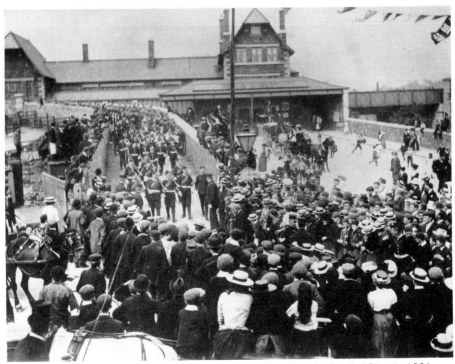

KENDAL STATION. The volunteers returning from the Boer War in South Africa in 1901.

THE KENDAL BAND of the Westmorland Rifle Volunteers in the Castle ruins, c. 1860.

DURING THE FIRST WORLD WAR the Duke of Lancaster's Own Yeomanry were stationed in Kendal on what was the County Showfield. The horse lines were in the open and the horses were fastened with a rope to the ground. During their stay in Kendal, dispatch riders were converted from horses to motor cycles and members of the Westmorland Motor Cycle Club assisted with their training.

THE 34TH WEST LANCASHIRE CASUALTY CLEARING STATION recruited in Kendal and South Westmorland during the First World War. The photograph was taken in the Market Place outside the entrance to the Market Hall.

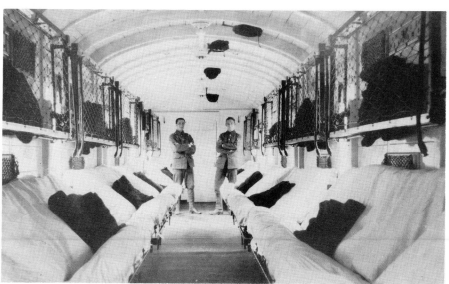

THE INTERIOR OF THE AMBULANCE TRAIN staffed by the 34th CCS. The Commanding Officer was Lieutentant Colonel Cockill, the Kendal Medical Officer of Health.

THE STRAMONGATE SCHOOL was used as a VAD Hospital during the First World War. The photograph shows the nursing staff and some of the wounded soldiers. It must have been taken late in the war after America had decided to join the Allies.

WOUNDED SOLDIERS WITH WASHERWOMEN at the Public Baths in Allhallows Lane. The lady on the left holds a wooden dolly which was used to rotate the dirty washing in a dolly tub.

THE STAFF AND VOLUNTEER SEWING LADIES repairing linen and uniforms at the Stramongate Hospital.

MEN OF THE 4TH BATTALION, THE BORDER REGIMENT during physical training instruction in the Castle ruins prior to departing for India in the First World War.

THE CENOTAPH IN THE MARKET PLACE was unveiled on 1 July 1921 by the local MP, Colonel Weston. A large crowd attended, including local schoolchildren, and an organ was brought on a flat cart to play for the hymn singing.

THE DRUMMERS OF 'D' COMPANY, the 4th Battalion, the Border Regiment arriving at the Cenotaph for an Armistice Day service in the late 1930s.

'D' COMPANY of the 4th Battalion, the Border Regiment waiting for the train at Kendal station in September 1939 after mobilization.

THE LOCAL HOME GUARD (Dad's Army) outside the Parish Hall.

THE HOME GUARD marching past the parish church in 1941.

ARMISTICE DAY, November 1943. In the background is the air raid shelter which was erected in the Market Place. The trumpeters of the Home Guard can be seen on the right playing the 'Last Post'.

SALUTE THE SOLDIER WEEK was held in May 1944 and a detachment of WRACs were in the parade. The photograph was taken on the New Road by Miller Bridge.

BREN GUN CARRIERS IN THE PARADE passing the saluting base at the Town Hall. W. Fulton Pennington was Mayor and Pat O'Neil Chief Constable.

ST JOHN AMBULANCE BRIGADE outside their headquarters in Sandes Avenue before joining the parade. On the left is superintendent Robert Wiper.

A CIVIC RECEPTION in the Committee Room in the Town Hall for ex-prisoners-of-war returned from German prison camps.

A CIVIC RECEPTION in the Mayor's Parlour in the Town Hall for ex-prisoners-of-war returned from Japanese prison camps. Mayor W. Fulton Pennington with the Mayoress is in the centre.

THE KENDAL BOROUGH POLICE FORCE at the turn of the century. The Chief Constable is sitting between Inspector J. Smith and Sergeant R. Coulter.

SUPERINTENDENT NOTMAN of the Westmorland County Police on the New Road outside the Catholic church.

AN AUXILIARY FIRE SERVICE was established at the start of the Second World War to assist regular fire brigades to deal with fires started by enemy bombing raids. This photograph was taken at the fire station on Aynam Road.

AT THE TURN OF THE CENTURY the Kendal Borough Council maintained a horse-drawn fire engine. Only one or two permanent men were employed, the remainder were volunteers. The photograph taken behind Stricklandgate House includes the members of the Watch Committee.

THE VOLUNTEER CREW OF AN AUXILIARY PUMP on Rinkfield. The wagon belongs to S. Downham and Son who were builders in Gillinggate. Local tradesmen's vehicles had to be used until enough fire engines became available.

THE MEMBERS OF THE KENDAL BOROUGH POLICE FORCE went on an outing to Southport in 1927 in a 'K' Bus. To avoid leaving the town unprotected, half the force went one week and the remainder the following week.

MEMBERS OF THE ROYAL OBSERVER CORPS at their post on the top of the hill behind Aikrigg Farm on Parkside Road.

SECTION SEVEN

Religion and Education

THE LADIES OF THE SUNDAY AFTERNOON CLASS at the Gillinggate Mission.

ST GEORGE'S CHAPEL IN THE MARKET PLACE was built in 1754 and demolished in 1855. The chapel was upstairs, and on the ground floor were three shops. Below was the town's dungeon and commodious vaults for storage of wines and spirits. A covered market hall was built on the site but upon the erection of the new market hall it was converted into a Free Library. This was demolished when the Carnegie Library was built in Stricklandgate in 1909.

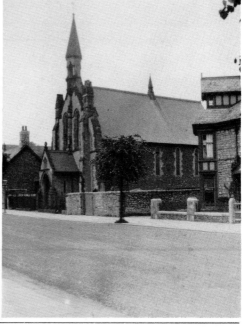

ST JOHN'S PRESBYTERIAN CHURCH was erected in Sandes Avenue in 1898. It was demolished in the 1970s and the adjoining hosiery factory was extended over the site. Unfortunately, this firm (E.W. Thomson) was taken over and the business moved away from Kendal. The whole site has been cleared and is awaiting development.

ST GEORGE'S CHURCH was built in 1840, replacing as a place of worship St George's chapel in the Market Place. The two spires became unsafe in the 1920s and the top portions were removed. More recently the remainder of the spires have been removed to roof level.

THE ROMAN CATHOLIC CHURCH AND PRESBYTERY were erected on the New Road in 1836 and dedicated to the Holy Trinity and St George. When the lower part of Black Hall Road was built the convent was demolished. The Presbytery has also been rebuilt.

THE JOB PENNINGTON MEMORIAL CHAPEL on Low Fellside was erected by public subscription in 1899. The adjoining school room was built in 1938 and the photograph shows W. Fulton Pennington at the stone-laying ceremony.

THE FOUNDATION STONE for the Sandylands Methodist church was laid by Mrs Thomas Pearson on 27 August 1953. The Revd Robert Armstrong was the superintendent minister and the mayor was Councillor Tom O'Loughlin. Previously the Methodists in that area had worshipped in a room known as the Longpool Mission above a wholesale newsagents. The church has been extended and altered several times since, most recently in 1983, and houses a very active Methodist community.

QUEEN SALOTE OF TONGA leaving the Stricklandgate Methodist church. She was in England for the coronation of Queen Elizabeth II.

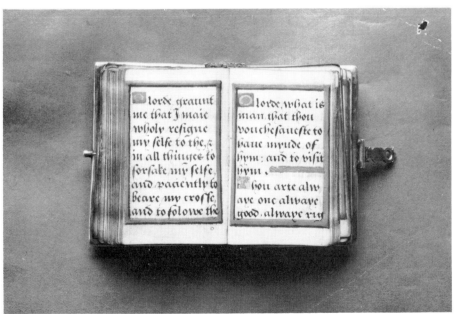

QUEEN KATHERINE PARR'S BOOK OF DEVOTIONS which is kept in a special safe in the Mayor's Parlour. Katherine Parr was probably born at Kendal Castle and was the sixth and surviving wife of Henry VIII. The book is one of the few surviving relics of the queen and was purchased by public subscription in 1936.

KENDAL GRAMMAR SCHOOL was founded in 1525. The building in the photograph was opened on 1 January 1889 by Sir James Whitehead who was Lord Mayor of London. There have been many extensions over the years.

BOARDERS WERE ACCOMMODATED until the Second World War and the photograph shows the dining room.

THE CHILDREN'S SPORTS in Abbot Hall Recreation Ground have been an annual event since the end of last century. All competitors receive a bag of sweets.

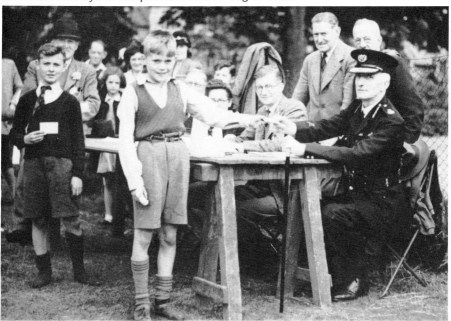

PRIZE WINNERS AT THE ABBOT HALL SPORTS collecting their vouchers from the Chief Constable, Pat O'Neil. Also seated at the table is Alfred Wainwright, at that time Chief Assistant in the Borough Treasurer's Department.

THE INFANTS' CLASS at St Thomas's School in 1914.

PUPILS RECEIVING WOODWORK INSTRUCTION in the workshop at the Friends School in Stramongate. This school was founded in 1698 and had an excellent preparatory and separate boarding house for younger boys. The school closed in the 1930s.

SECTION EIGHT

Royal and Civic Occasions

GUARD OF HONOUR OUTSIDE THE TOWN HALL on the occasion of the visit by Princess Christian on 28 April 1906 to celebrate the twenty-first anniversary of the Mary Wakefield Music Festival.

THE CHIEF CONSTABLE WITH REGULAR AND SPECIAL CONSTABLES in the Market Place prior to the arrival of Princess Christian.

SCENE OUTSIDE THE TOWN HALL before the arrival of the Princess by car to receive the Loyal Address from the Mayor.

THE PRINCE OF WALES PAID A VISIT in 1927 and is seen being presented with a pair of 'K' Shoes on the platform at the Town Hall. Note the reporter with his pad at the right of the picture.

THE PRINCE OF WALES inspecting First World War veterans who were on parade between the top of Finkle Street and the Town Hall. On completion of his visit to Kendal the Prince proceeded to Heversham to open the new by-pass which was called Prince's Way.

ALDERMAN W.H. STABLES LAID THE FOUNDATION STONE for the development of six bungalows at Crescent Green for the Mayor of Kendal's Fund for the Aged and Infirm on 3 December 1953. He had founded the charity in 1947 when he was mayor. Left to right: W.H. Stables, Revd David Prince, Tom Whiteside, Tom O'Loughlin (mayor), Mrs O'Loughlin (mayoress), George Jackson, Mrs Mona Pennington, Mrs Mildred Stables.

MRS MARY NOBLE handing over the keys of Noble's Rest to the mayor, Councillor N.F. Wilson in 1929. The gift was in memory of her husband Dr Sam Noble, and the park was originally intended for the old and the young. The Kendal Rugby Union Football Club had used the field for many years before moving to Mints Feet. At that time it was known as Maudes Meadow.

THE MAIN STREETS WERE DECORATED for the coronation of King George V. England was a major power in the world and proud of her Empire.

YOUNGSTERS, obviously enjoying themselves, admire the decorations at the top of Finkle Street looking towards the Town Hall.

HER MAJESTY QUEEN ELIZABETH II paid an official visit to Kendal in 1956. The Lord Lieutenant is saluting Her Majesty as she leaves the Town Hall with the mayor, Councillor Billy Gould. Prince Philip and the Town Clerk, Mr Harry Jones, can be seen in the background.

THE QUEEN AND PRINCE PHILIP IN THE COUNCIL CHAMBER being shown the town's regalia by the mayor and town clerk.

THE ROYAL CAVALCADE ENTERED THE TOWN from the south and this welcoming arch was erected on Milnthorpe Road.

ON THE CONCLUSION OF HER VISIT to Kendal the Queen moved on into the Lake District through this arch on Windermere Road.

THEIR ROYAL HIGHNESSES THE DUKE AND DUCHESS OF YORK at the 'K' Shoe Factory, Netherfield on 5 April 1935. On the left is Mr Leslie Somervell and on the right Mr Arnold Somervell. At that time the factory was owned by the Somervell Brothers.

THE LORD MAYOR OF LONDON, SIR JAMES WHITEHEAD, on the balcony of the Town Hall on the occasion of his admission as a Freeman of the Borough on 12 September 1889. He was the first person to receive the award.

THE KENDAL CO-OPERATIVE SOCIETY'S FLOATS in the Co-operative Depot in Beezon Road before joining the parade celebrating the coronation of Queen Elizabeth II. The floats advertised Penguin umbrellas and Spel detergent, both CWS products.

THE MAYOR, COUNCILLOR J.F. KNOWLES, the deputy mayor, Councillor E. Jones, and the town clerk, Mr Harold Rhodes, leading the procession into the parish church for a service of thanksgiving on the occasion of the Silver Jubilee of King George V and Queen Mary in 1935.

GIRL GUIDES CELEBRATING EMPIRE DAY in the Castle ruins in the early 1930s.

SECTION NINE

Street Scenes

LOOKING SOUTH DOWN HIGHGATE before the arrival of the motor car.

MALT KILN COTTAGES AND GLEBE COTTAGE on the Kirkland side of Nether Bridge. The gap between was the entrance to the old ford across the Kent. The Malt Kiln Cottages were demolished in 1906, the Glebe Cottage much later.

FARMERS' WIVES with their baskets of home-grown produce in Stramongate in the 1920s.

KIRKLAND FROM NETHER BRIDGE. The Malt Kiln Cottages have been demolished. A Model 'T' Ford is approaching the bridge.

LOWER STRICKLANDGATE before Sandes Avenue was built in 1887. The house behind the lamp belonged to Mr Sandes and was demolished to make the entrance to Sandes Avenue. The iron balconies can still be seen on the shop in Stricklandgate. The property leading to the County Offices is virtually unchanged.

YARDS were a feature of Kendal, and although they were numbered they were generally known by the name of the inn at the entrance or the owner of the property in the yard. The photograph was taken looking through the arch from Stricklandgate of Yard 44, White Lion Yard.

YARD 62, STRICKLANDGATE was known as Elephant Yard. C. Armstrong and Son, Practical Black and White Smiths, were in this yard.

STRICKLANDGATE before 1909 when the property behind the lamp was demolished to make way for the new Carnegie Library.

LOOKING UP STRICKLANDGATE from in front of the field now occupied by the County Offices. The building by the horse and cart was demolished in 1887 to make the entrance into Sandes Avenue.

LOOKING NORTH ALONG APPLEBY ROAD from outside the Duke of Cumberland Inn. Houses have been built on the right and entrances made to Sandylands Road and the Auction Mart.

LOOKING TOWARDS THE TOWN ALONG APPLEBY ROAD. Houses have been built on the right hand side.

LOOKING SOUTH DOWN KIRKLAND from outside the parish church. All the buildings on the left have been demolished.

A BUSY SCENE IN THE MARKET PLACE before the arrival of the motor car. Car parking ceased, except for the disabled, upon completion of the pedestrianization scheme in 1991.

J. HESLOP, UPHOLSTERER AND FRENCH POLISHER in Yard 67, Black Hall Yard, Stricklandgate. This yard was well used by pedestrians as a through route to Stramongate.

LOOKING UP YARD 23 TO STRAMONGATE. The properties in this yard have been renovated and are occupied as a small shopping precinct with access to the New Road.

THE STREET MARKET IN STRAMONGATE in the days when farmers brought their produce to Kendal by horse and trap. The horses were stabled at local inns.

FARMERS ARRIVING AT THE MARKET HALL with the produce which was sold by their wives from benches in the hall.

THE STEPS AT THE HEAD OF COLLIN CROFT give access to Beast Banks. The dwellings in the croft have been modernized by the Civic Society with the help of grants from the local authority.

THE SALVATION ARMY TEMPLE in Black Hall Yard. All the property in this photograph has been demolished.

MARKET STALLS AND FARMER'S TRAP in Highgate opposite the Town Hall.

THE STREET MARKET IN HIGHGATE. This is the main route through the town and as an integral part of the one way system is usually fully occupied by two lanes of traffic. Street markets are now restricted to the Market Place and Stramongate with the occasional stall on the New Road.

J. HENRY HOGG'S PHOTOGRAPHIC STUDIO and the Strickland's town house in Stricklandgate. The house was converted into the main post office in 1930. The studio has been altered many times by a series of occupiers but is now McDonalds.

A BUSY SCENE IN THE MARKET PLACE in the 1920s. Flowers on the War Memorial suggest that it is November. There were no traffic wardens to control the indiscriminate parking.

THE COBBLED YARDS IN HIGHGATE went down to the Waterside. There were many houses of character all demolished in the interests of slum clearance. This photograph shows a pleasant scene outside No. 2 in Yard 119, Highgate.

THE 'T' WELL ON OLD FELLSIDE about a hundred years ago. At times it must have been a major source of fresh water; at others a source of typhoid. The well was closed many years ago.

STRICKLANDGATE at the end of the nineteenth century. The only wheeled vehicles are a pram and a handcart. How different today! At that time the library was still at the entrance to the Market Place.

THE BUSY MARKET PLACE before the First World War. There doesn't appear to be any control over the market stalls, but cars are beginning to appear.

SECTION TEN

Miscellaneous

EMPLOYEES outside the premises adjoining the New Road of Arthur Simpson, Wood Carver, and Fawcett & Alexander, Mineral Water Manufacturers.

EARLY IN THE SECOND WORLD WAR there was an appeal for old aluminium pans for the aircraft industry. This photograph of the guides with the Gas Department hand cart was taken by the entrance to the Town Hall cellar in Lowther Street.

THE 1ST KENDAL (YWCA) GUIDES were obviously very successful with their collection of pans. The photograph was taken in the Old Shambles outside Brunskill & Farrer's Office.

EVACUEES ON KENDAL STATION in July 1944 after coming from the south of England to escape from the V1 and V2 rockets.

EVACUEES ON OXENHOLME STATION in December 1944 waiting to return to Tyneside.

THE KENDAL ST JOHN AMBULANCE TEAM, winners of the Crossfield Challenge Shield in 1901.

JACK ROBINSON WITH THE ST JOHN AMBULANCE CADETS on Stramongate School Field in 1927.

THE BOROUGH COUNCIL, as Urban Sanitary Authority, built an Isolation Hospital in 1882 on Parkside Road for fever and other infectious diseases. The buildings were known locally as the Sanatorium and patients were admitted from adjoining areas. The photograph shows the Medical Officer of Health, Dr W.B. Cockill, with the nursing staff. After the Second World War the buildings were converted into temporary accommodation to meet the housing shortage.

THE MEMORIAL HOSPITAL built in 1870 in memory of Mrs James Cropper was closed in 1908 when the patients were moved by members of the St John Ambulance Brigade to a new Westmorland County Hospital. This hospital was closed in 1991 when it was replaced by the Westmorland General Hospital on Burton Road.

PATRONS WITH THE BARMAIDS at the side entrance to the County Hotel in Wildman Street.

BETWEEN THE WARS it was the practice of the mayor to raise money during his year of office to provide parcels for poor families at Christmas. Meat and groceries were sorted in the Bindloss Room and the parcels were delivered by volunteers in local tradesmen's vans. The mayor, Alderman W. Cleasby can be seen in his shirt sleeves in the centre of the photograph.

TO CELEBRATE THE CO-OPERATIVE CENTENARY in 1912, there was a parade through the main streets to Town View Field on Windermere Road where games and competitions were held and the children were given bags of buns and cakes and commemorative mugs. The girls on this cart are polishing spoons with Pelaw Polish.

THE LADIES DEPARTMENT at Waterloo House in Finkle Street when it was the central store for the Kendal Co-operative Society.

THE TOLL BAR COTTAGE north of Kendal on the road to Windermere. The road to the left was to Bowness via Crook. The cottage was demolished and a roundabout constructed when the Kendal by-pass was completed.

VIEW OF PARKSIDE ROAD CEMETERY from the bridge over the canal at the gasworks. The cemetery was consecrated in 1854 and this photograph was taken by J. Henry Hogg at the end of the nineteenth century.

COWS IN THE RIVER KENT at Nether Bridge. The entrance to the old ford in Kirkland was used as access.

ACKNOWLEDGEMENTS

Over the last thirty years so many people have donated photographs to our collection that it is impossible to mention them individually. Without their interest and assistance this book would never have been published and their kindness is gratefully acknowledged.